Robert

The True Story of a Child Rapist and Serial Killer

by C.L. Swinney

Robert Black

The True Story of a Child Rapist and Serial Killer

by C.L. Swinney

ISBN-13: 978-1517624156

ISBN-10: 1517624150

Copyright and Published
(2015)
by

RJ Parker Publishing, Inc.

Published in Canada
(British English)

Copyrights

This book is licensed for your personal enjoyment only. All rights reserved. No part of this publication can be reproduced or transmitted in any form or by any means without prior written authorization from *RJ Parker Publishing, Inc*. The unauthorized reproduction or distribution of a copyrighted work is illegal. Criminal copyright infringement, including infringement without monetary gain, is investigated by the FBI and is punishable by fines and federal imprisonment.

FBI ANTI-PIRACY WARNING

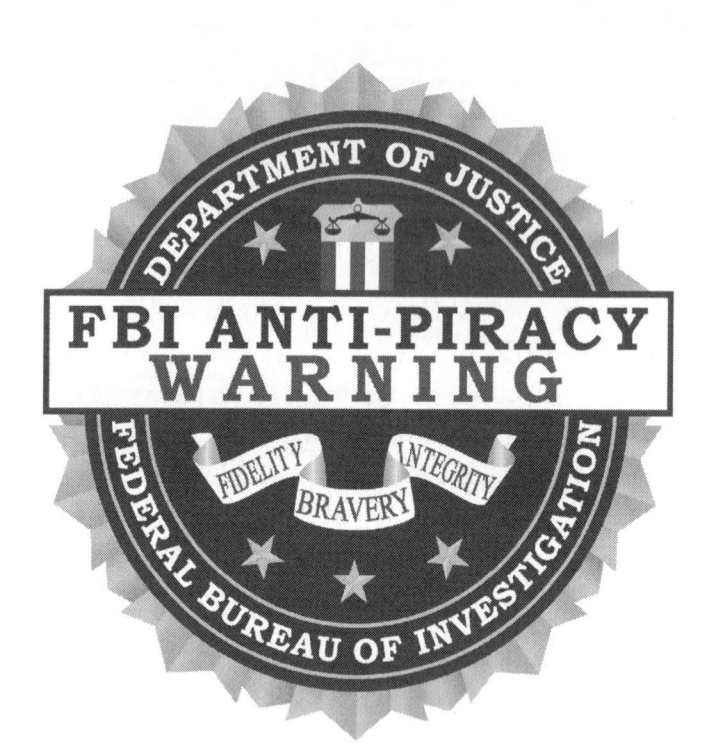

Table of Contents

Prologue..7

Chapter One..11

Chapter Two...31

Chapter Three...41

Chapter Four...51

Chapter Five..61

Chapter Six..69

Chapter Seven..73

Chapter Eight..83

Chapter Nine..101

Chapter Ten..107

Chapter Eleven...119

Chapter Twelve..127

NOTE:

This book was written using **British English** and therefore words may appear to some to be spelled incorrectly. For example, we use realise not realize, offence instead of offense.

Prologue

Jennifer Cardy

Ballinderry, County Antrim, Northern Ireland, August 12, 1981

Nine-year-old Jennifer Cardy asked her folks if she could go for a bike ride to her friend's house wanting to play. They discussed her request and figured since where she wanted to go was close by, and she'd done the trip several times prior, she should be allowed to go. She left her home in Ballinderry, County Antrim in Northern Ireland, and pedaled off to meet and play with her friend. Jennifer never made it to her destination. Strangely, none of the townsfolk recalled seeing her leave the area on her bicycle, on foot, or perhaps by vehicle.

Jennifer's parents and siblings went on foot, then later in their vehicle, to search for her. After a few minutes, Jennifer's bicycle was located within a mile of her home. The bike was along a major road, and it appeared whoever left the bike tried to disguise it (although feebly) with bushes. The location of where her bike was found, suggests she was headed in the right direction to play with her friend. But the fact she was nowhere to be seen, and her bicycle was found and appeared slightly covered by bushes, her family, and later the police, believe foul play had occurred.

Lisburn Royal Police Department, of the Police Service of Northern Ireland, was notified that Jennifer was missing. They began an exhaustive search for her and sent two officers to the location where her bicycle was recovered in an effort to gather evidence or clues as to what happened. Citizens in the immediate area were contacted and interviewed by the police. Not one person could say they saw her dump her bicycle, walk away, or get into a vehicle. It's as though she vanished into thin air. Her disappearance left the community and her family in a state of shock; they began to pray for her safe return.

Six days later, everyone's greatest fear became a reality as Jennifer's body was located at McKee's Dam near Hillsborough, County Down. A jogger had noticed her body in the lake and called the police. Carefully, her body was retrieved from the lake and she was briefly examined at the scene. The forensic pathologist on scene observed signs of sexual abuse and determined Jennifer likely died from drowning - meaning she was alive when she was tossed into the lake.

Her case baffled local law enforcement and frustration sank in as no evidence, either from the original kidnapping or in and around the location where her bike was recovered, was obtained. In 1981, traffic cameras were non-existent. In addition, not a single witness was available. Without evidence, witnesses, or leads, the police had no chance of identifying a suspect for Jennifer's murder. Her family was left trying to collect themselves, to attempt to put their lives back in order. Unbelievably, they'd have to wait nine years before a suspect is identified and later charged in the murder of Jennifer Cardy. No one – perhaps not even the killer - was prepared for how much damage and fear would come in those nine years.

Jennifer with her bike, 1981

Chapter One

Grangemouth, Scotland, April 21, 1947

A male child was born to a young unmarried woman, Jessie Hunter Black. She refused to list the father's name on the birth certificate. Jessie named the boy Robert, but within a few months, she placed him up for foster care. Suitable parents were interviewed until Robert was placed with Margaret and Jack Tulip. The Tulips had fostered children previously, but they were in their fifties and would have their hands full with young Robert Black.

At the tender age of five, Robert experienced his first major life tragedy. Jack, the only man he'd known as a father, suddenly died. Robert claimed to have no memory of Jack, but many have suggested and it was believed, based on bruising located on Robert as a child, that Jack physically abused Robert. Robert denied being physically abused, but also could not account for how he managed to be so bruised. With Jack passing away, it left

Margaret to take on both parenting roles. The death certainly had an effect on Robert - even though he claims otherwise - because his behavior began to deteriorate rapidly once Jack passed away.

Margaret, struggling to keep the reins on Robert, would lock him in a room in their small house when he acted out. She'd also pull down his trousers and underwear and spank him with a belt.

Some nights "Robbie" thought a monster lived under his bed and lay in wait to get him. He suffered a recurring nightmare involving a "big hairy monster" in a cellar full of water. Robert would wake from these nightmares and find his bed wet. He later said the bed wetting embarrassed him, but it also meant he'd be beaten by Margaret for "his bad behavior."

At age eight, according to Robert, he began truly experiencing his own sexuality. He placed items in his anus, and felt, at least at times, that he should have been born a girl. He would keep these thoughts hidden deep within, however. Unfortunately, they'd later come out in a series of violent episodes that would shock the conscience. Robert later said his sexual exploration actually began closer to the age of five. He became fascinated with his genitals and recalled showing them to a girl close to his age. Left unchecked, Robert would continue to experiment with his, and eventually others', bodies.

Primary school while growing up with a single parent proved difficult for Robert, or "Smelly Robbie Tulip," as the kids called him. Known for being aggressive at times, but also carefree, Robert perplexed those around him. School work did not challenge him, but the teachers and other students didn't quite know what to think of him. Not too many kids would admit they were friends with Robert. He'd say later that he preferred being a "free spirit" and didn't need any friends.

"A bit of a loner, but tended to bully smaller kids," his school mate Colin McDougall said of Robert. Robert preferred to spend time with children younger than him. The children said this was because he was bigger than them and he would use his size to intimidate them. Colin McDougall added, "We had a gang, but he insisted on being the leader of his own gang. The members in his gang were always a couple of years younger than him."

Another of Robert's school mates, Jimmy Minnes, told a story of Robert beating up a younger boy who had an artificial leg, "He (Robert) gave the poor lad a terrible hammering. He just jumped on top of him as he was walking over the bridge to school one day. Robert punched and kicked him for no reason." These random violent encounters were typical of Robert as a young child, but his behavior never got addressed. Seeing accountability for his aggressive and questionable behavior never happened, Robert chose to keep pushing the envelope and experimenting to see what he could get away with.

At the age of eleven, Robert was dealt another serious blow as Margaret passed away. She was the last shred of family Robert had. His biological mother had given him up for adoption, and now both of his foster parents were dead. Many years later, when Robert reached adulthood, he learned his biological mother eventually married and had four children. She never attempted to see him after giving him up, and Robert never met his half-siblings. This point would come up again - after it was too late - and it is obvious Robert had a difficult time learning his mother abandoned him and would not let him see his half-siblings.

Upon the passing of Margaret, Robert moved to the Redding Children's Home in Falkirk, an orphanage close to where he'd been born. He immediately began behaving oddly and the kids there called him "Smelly Robbie." Robert did not like to take showers or baths, a trend throughout his life. Students and staff reported when Robert argued and fought with other children and had bruises on his body (although no one admitted they knew where the bruises came from). Robert himself would be asked about the bruises, he answered, "I don't know where they come from." Since the age of five, people around Robert noticed his body had bruises, and now, six years later, his body again had bruising. Some suggested Robert, although being a bully and an aggressive kid, was also being physically abused.

A local officer, Sandy Williams, later described Robert as a "wild wee laddie" who "didn't give a damn - no respect for authority. He had a dangerous spirit," and "needed a smack round the ear to keep him in line." Robert, at least while living with the Tulips, never got in real trouble. He acted up at school, had shoving matches with local kids, and bullied younger kids, but the most he got from Williams was a serious verbal reprimand for cursing in front of women.

At the age of twelve, Robert crossed the line and finally grabbed the attention of officials. He and two other boys observed a young girl walking in a field near Robert's home in Falkirk. Without hesitation, they attacked her and held her down while each of them tried to put their penises in her vagina. Robert said none of them could get an erection, so they left her crying in the field. Vague details about the incident were reported to the police. However, none of the boys were charged with attempted rape. Concerned about Robert's activity and alarming tendencies, officials determined he should be moved to another Children's Home in Mussleburgh.

While at the orphanage, Robert experienced a change in roles. For approximately two years, a male member of the staff - now dead - regularly sexually abused Robert. The abuser had been abusing another boy, but that boy had to leave the school because he was too old. The sexual predator staff member forced his victim to find him a new victim. The other boy victim recommended Robert. Robert recalled the abuse occurring as follows, the man, he said "made me put his penis in my mouth, touch him, you know... He did try to bugger me once, but he couldn't get an erection."

These events confirmed for Robert that sex equated with dominance and submission. Robert, now a victim, empathised and identified with his abuser. Based on what he'd been exposed to, Robert concluded he could take what he wanted without regard for other people's feelings. He never reported the abuse but later talked about it while being interviewed. When he recalled the story, some twenty years later, the look on his face suggested the abuse he experienced meant nothing to him, almost like being sexually abused by a trusted person was completely normal for him.

Staff at the home found a local middle school willing to enroll Robert even though he'd developed a reputation for being a bully. He enjoyed swimming, but he still did not hang around kids his age (he preferred younger people) and had very few friends. He tried out as a footballer and demonstrated great skills. Unfortunately, his poor eyesight forced him from the team. Not being able to play a sport he loved negatively impacted Robert. Robert continued to swim and developed a reputation of being a great swimmer. He used the solid reputation to land a job as a lifeguard. There were two local pools that he worked at near the orphanage. Sadly, these pools would become a crime zone some twenty years later.

In 1962, when Robert was fifteen years old, the Children's Home sent him out on the streets. He struck out to find a life of his own with severe psychological stress based on the fact he'd been left for adoption by his mother, never knew his father, his adoptive parents abused him and died when he was young, he bounced around orphanages, and a trusted staff member sexually abused him for two years.

Surprisingly, he found a job as a delivery boy and rented a room in Greenock, near Glasgow. After his apprehension, he told investigators that he molested thirty to forty girls while working this first job. It does not appear a single one of the molestations was reported to law enforcement. Robert, becoming more devious and arguably more demented, continued his path of sexual deviancy without anyone knowing the wiser.

At the age of seventeen years old, Robert admitted to asking a seven-year-old girl if she wanted to go with him to a park to see some kittens. The little girl agreed and followed Robert. He ended up taking her to a deserted building, strangled her unconscious, and then lied down next to her. He then masturbated and ejaculated on her unconscious body. Robert finished his sexual perversion act and left the girl - dead or alive - in the building without a care. Unbelievably, the victim, stunned and bleeding, was found by a passerby.

The illegal and despicable things Robert did to the little girl, once reported to the police, caused him to get arrested. Robert, after being found guilty of the act, did not serve jail or prison time. All he received for what he'd done was a verbal admonishment. When recounting the rape, Robert told Ray Wyre, "I took her inside and I held her down on the ground with my hand round her throat... I must have half-strangled her or something because she was unconscious...When she was quiet I took her knickers off and I lifted her up so as I was holding her behind her knees and her vagina was wide open and I poked my finger in there once."

Robert left the area and moved back to Grangemouth. He found a job with a construction company, found a room to rent, and began a relationship with his first (and only) girlfriend, Pamela Hodgson. Robert never knew love until meeting Pamela. After a few months, he asked her to marry him. She initially said yes to the proposal; however, she broke off the engagement and left Robert abruptly. There has never been an explanation as to why Pamela left him the way she did. Robert said Pamela leaving him, the stinging rejection, crushed him inside. Robert would lash out because of the rejection, and his behavior became drastically worse. In fact, in 1992, when

Robert was served with ten summonses (he'd been in custody since 1990 at this time) for three murders, he blurted to the officers, "tell Pamela she's not responsible for all of this." Clearly, her rejection stunned him and contributed to the creation of a monster. It's been well documented that serial killers, when dealing with rejection and broken hearts, commit terrible acts trying to cover their own grief.

Late in the year of 1966, the manifestation of Robert's sexual desires appeared again when he molested a nine-year-old girl. She happened to be the daughter of his landlord at the time. She eventually told her parents what Robert had done. They did not report him to the police but demanded he leave their home at once. This, as the numerous other unreported incidents, cemented in Robert's mind that his actions, illegal and immoral, were acceptable because he had no repercussions.

Robert left the area and moved to Kinlochleven, somewhat close to where he spent his childhood. He took a room with a couple who had a seven-year-old daughter. Robert, unable to resist or control himself, molested her as well. The police were notified of the sexual abuse leading to Robert's arrest. He received a one-year sentence of borstal training at Polmont. Borstal training is a youth detention center in the United Kingdom designed for serious youth offenders. The time Robert spent at the borstal must have been difficult. When asked about it, he refused to talk about his experience. I shudder considering what goes on in such a facility, and the fact Robert, normally open about most things in his life, won't talk about it, seems like whatever happened there certainly bothered him.

On his release from the borstal, Robert moved from Scotland to London. He stopped abusing young girls because he developed an interest in child pornography. When he was apprehended years later, when he'd just kidnapped another little girl, police obtained a search warrant for his home. They discovered hundreds of porno magazines and fifty child porn videos. Although inhumane, these videos and magazines preoccupied Robert. He spent time with these sexual devices instead of working the streets looking for potential targets.

While in London, Robert found work as a swimming pool attendant. No one in London knew about his issues while a lifeguard years prior. In this new job, Robert would go underneath the pool, remove the lights, and watch young girls as they swam. Soon after, a young girl complained that Robert had touched her. Robert did not deny the girl's claim. No official charges were brought, but he was immediately fired. Yet another documented criminal act by Robert, sexually driven, went unreported and, therefore, no accountability followed.

Robert developed a second passion while residing in London - that of playing darts. He became a reasonable player and was well-known among amateur darts circuits. Darts world champion (at the time) Eric Bristow knew Robert vaguely, remembering him as a "loner" who never seemed to have a girlfriend.

Michael Collier, the former owner of Baring Arms Pub in Islington where Robert played darts, often said, "For all the years he drank in my pub you would never call him a mate. He drank pints of lager Shandy, but he never got involved in rounds. When he wasn't playing darts, he just stood by the fruit machine. Robert was a bit of a wind-up merchant and enjoyed irritating people, particularly women...He never talked about himself and he never spoke of his interests or joined in conversations."

In 1972, Robert met Eddie and Kathy Rayson at a pub in Stamford Hill, north London. Robert actually spoke with the Raysons, which is interesting because he talked to so few people. He eventually told them he needed a place to stay. The Raysons had space in their attic, but Eddie wasn't sure about letting Robert stay with them. Eddie said he felt something wasn't right about Robert. However, Kathy described Robert as a "big softie," and they agreed to let him stay. After Robert's second conviction in 1994, Eddie Rayson remembered him as "a perfect tenant. He always paid the rent on time and never caused us any problems." Robert ate with the couple and their children (who had nicknamed him 'Smelly Bob'). The kids would play cards or listen to music with Robert in his attic room. Eddie Rayson even stated Robert "was a bit like a father to me," but Robert never opened up to him. Eddie and Kathy's son, Paul, described Robert as "a bit odd, and as kids growing up, we called him names mainly because he smelled. But he was an ideal tenant." In fact, Paul continued, describing Robert as "more than just a tenant, but not what you would call a friend... not the sort of person you would ever be able to get close to, or would want to."

The Raysons told of a much different side of Robert. One of his passions was photography. They sometimes called Robert "David Bailey," a well-known photographer. But Robert did not take photographs that could be shared with the world. Robert would later tell Ray Wyre that one of his favorite pastimes involved video-recording children playing or taking snapshots of them in bathing suits. Robert would use these photos and videos to arouse himself. Interestingly to me is the fact the Raysons' children never alleged Robert touched or sexually abused them.

In 1976, Robert stepped away from playing darts and found a job as a van driver for a company named Poster Dispatch and Storage (PDS). Robert delivered posters throughout England and Scotland. This job suited him because he set his own schedule; the easy work and the long drives alone gave him time to think. Robert managed to drive for PDS for ten years; however, the company let him go because he'd been involved in so many accidents that their insurance skyrocketed. Nevertheless, shortly after being fired, PDS was bought by two people (two previous employers). The new owners re-hired Robert immediately because good drivers were hard to find. Fellow employees enjoyed having Robert around because he worked hard and volunteered for the long runs from London to Scotland, allowing them to stay local and spend more time with their families. Robert looked forward to the long runs because he'd often stop in the Midlands on his way back to see John Rayson (son of Kathy and Eddie) and John's new family. None of John's family ever alleged that Robert violated or sexually assaulted them.

Had the PDS owners ever looked in Robert's van, they may have had second thoughts about keeping him with the company. He kept various objects he'd use as masturbation tools - items he'd insert into his anus and masturbated while thinking of little girls - inside his work van. He would sometimes put an object in his anus and leave it there for the entire ride. Robert later told police that he'd get into the back of the van at night, dress in girl's clothing, usually swimming suits, and masturbate with various objects in his anus. He said he did this often. Robert believed this to be completely normal behavior.

Ray Wyre, a nationally recognized child protection expert in the United Kingdom, interviewed and worked with Robert after his apprehension. Wyre also pioneered the treatment of sexual offenders in the UK. Robert told Wyre that the image of the little girl he left for dead in the abandoned building, the one he strangled and masturbated on at the age of seventeen, constantly appeared in his thoughts. Wyre believed this incident, and the fact it continually played in Robert's mind, drove him to become a serial killer. Robert would repeat the scenarios (and murders) in an effort to fulfill the fantasy and finally resolve the anger and frustration in his head from the incident.

The death and destruction Robert left in his path while trying to rid his mind of the disturbing and haunting image of the young girl he left for dead after he'd sexually violated her would stretch on for many years. Families and communities would be ripped apart as Robert stalked, kidnapped, raped, and murdered young innocent girls. The following is the story of the victims of serial killer Robert Black.

Robert during an interview, 1990

Robert's home, 1990

Chapter Two

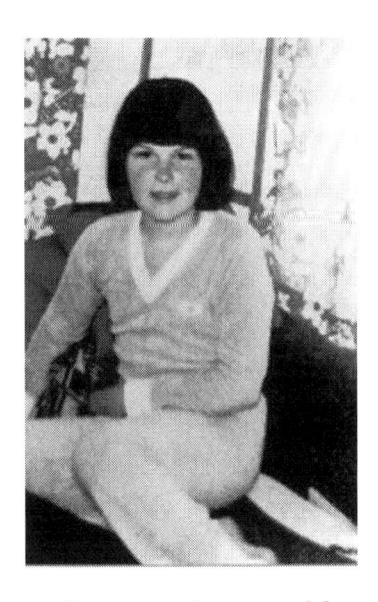

Susan Maxwell, Robert's second known victim, 1982

Tweed, England, July 30, 1982

On a blistering hot afternoon in Tweed, England, eleven-year-old Susan Maxwell asked her mother, Liz, if she could ride her bike to meet up with her friend, Alison Raeburn, to play tennis. She'd never asked to do this before, but she was eleven after all and felt she should be allowed to ride her bike.

A battle within Liz's head ensued because she was torn over a relatively simple question. On one hand, she was worried because Susan had never biked alone and the traffic in the area was heavy. On the other, Susan was getting older and letting her venture out on her own would help build her confidence. Liz finally agreed to let Susan go play tennis, but demanded she walk instead. It was a compromise of sorts, because Susan had also never walked alone. Liz was both nervous and excited seeing Susan, wearing her favorite yellow dress and carrying her tennis racket, walk out the front door.

The Maxwells lived in a modest farmhouse in Tweed, a small village on the English side of the English-Scottish border. Susan's tennis game was across the Scottish border in Coldstream, roughly two miles from her home. The path she told her mother she wanted to take would enable plenty of people who knew her to keep eyes on her. The tight-knit community looked out for each other. Certainly children were watched even closer because one never knew what sort of mischief they could get in.

Susan walked toward the border still miffed at not being able to ride her bike. After a few minutes, a farm worker she and her family knew, also headed to Coldstream, offered her a ride. Susan excitedly jumped in the man's truck and he dropped her off at the tennis courts where Alison was waiting. She told Alison all about how she ended up getting a ride and how her mother wouldn't let her ride her bike. Susan told Alison that she'd walk home after their game. During the game, both of the girls talked about getting together again the following day.

Around 4 p.m., Liz decided to drive to pick up Susan. She put her other smaller children in their car and began the short drive to the tennis courts.

Liz recalled, "She wasn't expecting me. But I thought, 'It's a very hot afternoon; after she's been playing tennis for an hour, she'll be hot and sticky and too tired to walk back.' So I put the wee ones in the back and we went over." Liz fully expected to find Susan along the road walking home, but she did not see her.

After not seeing Susan, Liz frantically responded to the Lennel Tennis Club. She did not see Susan there either. She drove up and down a few local streets, then decided she needed to call Alison's mother. Liz learned that Alison left Susan after their game, and Allison was already home.

"I started to panic then," said Liz, "And Fordyce (her husband) said to just phone the police straightaway."

The Northumberland Police Department was immediately contacted. Within minutes, they began searching for Susan and questioning people regarding her whereabouts. Many people had seen Susan that afternoon, including some who recalled seeing a little girl, dressed in yellow, swinging a tennis racket. Some said they saw her around the Tweed Bridge, but no one recalled seeing her after she went over the bridge into England.

A few people interviewed noticed seeing her around 4:30 in the evening. Oddly, no one reported seeing her after this time. In addition, nobody reported seeing a little girl being abducted. Within the blink of an eye, Susan literally disappeared.

Residents in the area banded together forming search parties looking for Susan. Most people involved assumed she'd been abducted. Volunteers showed up at the Northumbria Police Department eager to help. More than half of the locals in the town were involved in her search. Fordyce, Susan's father, spent most of his time joining the searches. The story remained in the news because the Maxwell family believed it would be helpful to keep pictures of Susan in the public's eye.

On August 13, two weeks after Susan went missing, and after Fordyce and Liz returned from a radio show they agreed to do in an effort to get everyone they could to hear about their missing daughter, the situation changed. When they got home, they noticed police officers waiting for them in front of their home.

"He (an officer) said they'd found a little girl. And I remember he wouldn't say the word 'dead'. He just said, 'This little girl is not alive.' And that was when the sort of coldness spread right through me," recalled Liz.

Arthur Meadows, a fellow some 250 miles away, had found what officials believed was Susan's body. She was next to a ditch (a lay-by) on the A518 road near Loxley, outside of Uttoxeter, in the Midlands.

Liz and Fordyce asked if they could see their daughter's body. The officer warned them that the weather had been very warm and her body had decomposed beyond recognition. They later chose not to see their daughter because they felt seeing her that way would be too much to handle.

Susan was identified by her dental records. The pathologist, due to the decomposition, was unable to determine her cause of death. The only clue was that Susan's panties had been removed. Her shorts were then replaced, her panties folded beneath her head. This stirred suspicion that the motive for the attack was sexual, but it was unclear what had happened to Susan. The Tweed community was shocked by the grisly discovery.

Staffordshire Police Department took over the investigation as Susan's remains were located in their jurisdiction. However, they worked closely with the Northumbria Police Department since she'd been abducted in their jurisdiction. Everyone involved with this case was disgusted and heartbroken. The support for the Maxwell family was grand, but all they wanted now was the killer to be caught and held to answer for what he'd done.

Witnesses of Susan's 'final walk' were re-questioned, and people who had been in the area where Susan's body had been found were located and interviewed. Photographs of Susan were widely distributed and a reconstruction of the abduction was staged in an effort to jog the memories of any potential witnesses. Hotels and caravan sites were visited by investigators. Anyone with possible ties to the case would be interviewed at length. Drivers from transport firms between Scotland and Staffordshire were contacted and interviewed. The police exhausted hundreds of leads hoping to gain answers, as well as closure, for the Maxwells.

One of the most promising leads came from Mark Ball, a psychiatric nurse, who claimed to have seen a little girl matching Susan's description leaving the area in a maroon-coloured Triumph 2000. He said the girl was carrying a tennis racket at the time he saw her leave. Police interviewed 19,000 drivers of maroon Triumphs and gathered no useful data; therefore, the lead was abandoned. The case remained open; however, none of the police departments were any closer to identifying a suspect for the brutal crime, and residents were obviously on edge.

The investigation stretched almost a full year with no results. They created a database and it became full with over a half a million hand-written index cards. Like the Yorkshire Ripper investigation, Susan's murder investigation overwhelmed the police based on the sheer amount of accumulated data. Meanwhile, as the Maxwells were left to pick up the pieces of their once happy home, the suspect would continue to search for more victims. Parents with small female children were worried sick that a killer could strike again.

Unfortunately, as with most serial killer cases, another murder did in fact take place. This second murder forced the re-opening of Susan's case, but another family had to experience a horrific loss. The investigation into someone killing little girls, however, would gain fresh legs.

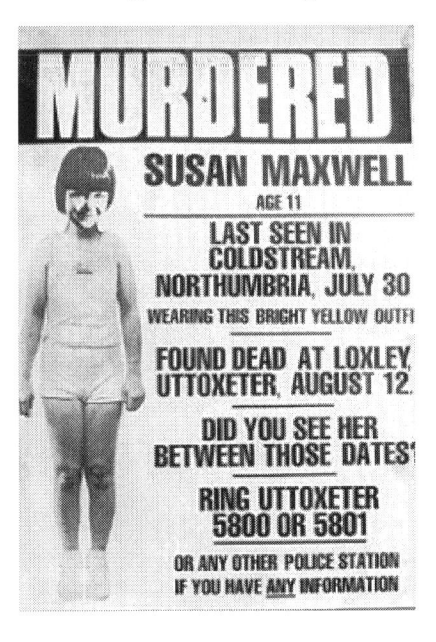

MURDERED

SUSAN MAXWELL
AGE 11

LAST SEEN IN COLDSTREAM, NORTHUMBRIA, JULY 30
WEARING THIS BRIGHT YELLOW OUTFIT

FOUND DEAD AT LOXLEY, UTTOXETER, AUGUST 12.

DID YOU SEE HER BETWEEN THOSE DATES?

RING UTTOXETER 5800 OR 5801

OR ANY OTHER POLICE STATION IF YOU HAVE ANY INFORMATION

Chapter Three

Caroline Hogg, Robert's third known victim, 1983

Portobello, Edinburgh, July 8, 1983

Five-year-old Caroline Hogg spent the afternoon with her mother at a friend's party. They'd just returned home and were getting ready to take her grandmother to the nearby bus stop. She asked her mother, Annette Hogg, if she could play a little longer after they dropped off her grandmother. Annette said she would think about it.

Caroline, her mother, and her grandmother drove to drop off Caroline's grandmother. They returned just before seven o'clock. Caroline, still full of energy, nagged her mother to let her go down the street to play a few more minutes before bed time. Caroline had been playing at the playground for years because it only required a short walk to get there. Annette, like most mothers would do, finally gave in and allowed Caroline five minutes of play time. Like Coldstream, Portobello is a small community where the residents all know each other. As an added precaution, Annette told Caroline over and over to never talk to strangers and reminded her that she was never allowed to go past the park to the permanent fairground, Fun City.

At 7:15 p.m., Annette sent her son, Stuart, to look for his sister. He meandered around a little, checked the park where she said she would be, but did not see Caroline. He returned home and told his mom that he could not find her. Annette stopped doing the dishes and began looking for Caroline.

Within a few minutes, panic set in, and the rest of the family began searching the area for signs of Caroline. They spent about forty-five minutes searching, even checking Fun City, before giving up and calling the police.

Many people had seen Caroline that night. Some of the sightings were of her and a man later identified as her abductor. At least three different citizens stated they saw Caroline holding hands with a "scruffy looking" man. They reported that the same man was observed watching the little girl (Caroline) while she played at the playground, and followed her closely when she left the playground and into Fun City, the place she absolutely could not go. The man paid for her to go on the children's roundabout (carousel). The man watched and smiled at her as she went around and around. When the ride was over, the young girl grabbed the man's hand, and they were seen walking out the back entrance of Fun City. The Hogg Family, upon hearing these statements, expected the worst for Caroline.

As the police had done in the previous summer (during Susan Maxwell's murder), the local police quickly set up search parties.

Within two days, the police had more than 600 volunteers searching for Caroline, or her remains. Within a week's time, over 2,000 people had joined the search. At the time, it was the largest search conducted in Scotland. Sadly, the results were negative. Neither the family nor the police had any idea that Caroline's kidnapper had taken her hundreds of miles south. Despite weeks of searching, no evidence of her abduction existed.

Unlike the Maxwells, Annette and John Hogg chose to speak only one time to the media. They had a difficult time knowing some unknown man had taken Caroline from them. They wanted to remain optimistic, but the facts made it near impossible to remain calm.

John Hogg begged to the abductor on live television, "Just bring her back... Please, let her come home."

Annette said to the kidnapper while sobbing, "We really miss her. I really miss her."

Superintendent Ronald Stalker candidly told the press, "I am afraid that all we have to say at this stage is that we have turned up nothing at all." This report frustrated the community. As days slipped by, investigators knew the longer the case went on, the less likely they'd find Caroline alive.

On July 18, 1983, Caroline's body was found in a ditch on the side of the road at Twycross in Leicestershire near to the A444, the road that goes from Northampton to Coventry. This was almost three hundred miles from where she'd been kidnapped. If you recall, Susan's body was also taken a long way from her home, but both Susan and Caroline's bodies were located within twenty-four miles of each other. Investigators were not sure if this was a coincidence or not. But, they knew they had two young female victims, taken a long way from their homes, and their bodies were found relatively close to each other.

Ten days had passed since the abduction. The long amount of time, coupled with the hot weather, led to Caroline's body being badly decomposed. Therefore, the cause of death, at least initially, was unknown. At the time, investigators identified her remains from a locket around her neck and a hair-band. Her body was completely naked, suggesting the motive was likely sexual, which was also similar to Susan's murder. This added a sexual element possibly connecting the two murders.

Because of the similarities in the murders of Susan and Caroline, it was decided by the Chief Constables of the four forces now involved - Northumbria (where Susan was abducted), Staffordshire (where Susan was found), Edinburgh (where Caroline was abducted), and Leicestershire (where Caroline was found) - that the investigation for the case would be a joint inquiry.

In July of 1983, Hector Clark, the Deputy Chief Constable of the Northumbria Police, was put in charge of the joint effort. He was told he needed to solve these homicides quickly with little evidence to work with and was ordered to see how or if computers could help solve the murders. It hadn't been since the Yorkshire Ripper investigation that computers were thought of as plausible tools for serial murder investigations. Many, including most of the force, were doubtful computers would break open these cases. The computerised revolution had not yet begun around the globe at this time.

The amount of data from the Susan Maxwell investigation proved to be massive. Clark thought if the data could be entered into a computer, the two murder cases could be reviewed more efficiently. It required transcribing all the manual files into a computer database, which would take months to accomplish. Clark then determined whatever data they had for Caroline's case would be entered into the same database (combining data from Susan's case and Caroline's case). However, his superiors determined too much time would be wasted on the data entry. Instead, a computer program for the Caroline Hogg investigation specifically went live and computerised, while the data from Susan's case remained manual.

In Portobello, witnesses at Fun City were interviewed while officers literally went house to house looking for leads or answers. Leicestershire Officers were ordered to sit (for several weeks) near the A444 taking down the registration numbers of cars that passed. Local Intelligence Officers (LIO's) from every force in the entire country were contacted and asked if they knew someone they thought could be a suspect in the murders of Susan and Caroline. Police were desperate but hoped someone working in law enforcement would know of a criminal with this sort of MO.

Houses of men, based on them being seen near or on the promenade and near Fun City the night Caroline vanished, were searched. People visiting the area on holiday, as far away as Australia, were asked by police to send rolls of their vacation film or photographs taken in Portobello at the time Caroline disappeared. They hoped an image may have been captured containing the killer. Police conducted a reconstruction of Caroline's last journey hoping, similar to Susan's case, to jog someone's memory. Parking tickets issued in Edinburgh were examined to see if any known criminals or sexual predators were in the area at the time of these murders. These investigative techniques were met with negative results.

An artist's impression of the 'scruffy man' was released to the public. More than

600 names were given to police after the sketch went public. Each and every one of the names needed to be checked, verified that they had no involvement, and marked off the list. The investigation of both murders continued at length, but little information had been learned. The mention of a possible serial killer had been made among line-staff officers, but administrative types kept the possibility quiet.

A local couple, Mr. and Mrs. Flynn, thought they witnessed Caroline's abduction. They said they saw a blue Ford Cortina, driven by a man resembling the 'scruffy man,' with a "scared-looking" young girl in it. According to police records, 20,000 drivers of blue Ford Cortinas were contacted and interviewed throughout the country. Unfortunately, as with the maroon Triumph in Susan's case, the lead turned out to be useless.

The Hogg Family and four local police departments were overwhelmed by these events and no one had been identified, either from evidence or leads, as a suspect. Meanwhile, the killer, growing more brazen and tormented in his mind, continued on his merry way. As the parties involved struggled to regain control of their own lives, and police desperately looked for a suspect, time seemingly came to a standstill. Three more gruelling years, with no answers, stumbled along before further disaster struck. A report surfaced indicating another young female child had been kidnapped.

Chapter Four

Sarah Harper, Robert's fourth known victim, 1986

Morley, Leeds, England, March 26, 1986

It was 8:00 p.m. and the TV show Coronation Street was ending. Jacki, ten-year-old Sarah Harper's mother, asked her children who could go to the corner shop to buy her a loaf of bread. Sarah, trying to be a big girl, volunteered. Jacki smiled, patted Sarah on the head, and gave her money for the bread. On her way out, Sarah picked up two empty lemonade bottles intending to get the deposit for turning them in. She left her home in Brunswick Place headed to K&M Stores on Peel Street. The distance from her home and the store was roughly one hundred and thirty yards.

Sarah walked to the store and went inside. The owner of the store, Mrs. Champaneri, later stated Sarah returned the glass lemonade bottles and bought a loaf of white bread. Mrs. Champaneri said she also bought two packets of crisps (wafers/cookies for us state-side). Sarah left the shop at 8:05 p.m. Two girls who knew Sarah said they had seen her walking home toward an alley they also used for years as a short cut. However, Sarah never returned home.

Around 8:15 p.m., Jacki began to worry. She knew the whole process of going to the store, buying the bread, and coming back should have taken around five minutes. Jacki wasn't completely freaked out however, because she figured Sarah would be in the alley eating a treat she didn't want her mom to see. Jacki sent Sarah's sister, Claire, out to look for her. Claire retraced the steps that she thought her sister would have taken, but did not find Sarah. Jacki and her family got in their car and began frantically searching for Sarah.

At approximately 9:00 p.m., the family alerted the police. As with any other missing child case, the police acted quickly, and a search for Sarah was initiated. Similar to the other cases, the search proved unsuccessful. Weeks would go by before anything would develop in Sarah's case. The family, on pins and needles, were worried sick about Sarah. Their worst fears became true on April 19, 1986.

David Moult told police he was walking his dog near the River Trent in Nottingham and noted "something floating in the water. I thought it was a piece of sacking, then the current turned it around, and I realised it was a body." Using a stick, Moult managed to drag the body over to the side of the river bank. He then called the police.

After an autopsy was conducted, it was determined that she entered the river near junction 24 of the M1 and was still alive at the time she went into the water. The pathologist described the injuries, which had been inflicted pre-mortem, as "terrible." As Ray Wyre later described it, "Sarah's assailant had violently explored both her vagina and her anus."

Jacki Harper, like Liz Maxwell, recalled the moment after being told of her daughter's body being discovered.

"All he [the officer] could say was 'Would you like to make a cup of tea?' And all I kept saying was 'Will you tell me what you have to tell me?' I knew why they were there - it was obvious. But he wouldn't tell me; he just kept going on about this bloody tea. All I wanted him to say was 'Yes, we've found her.'"

Terry Harper, Sarah's father and Jacki's ex-husband, identified his daughter's body. He would state, "It was worse than I ever dreamed of."

Hector Clark, involved with Susan and Caroline's cases, was aware of Sarah's case, but he did not believe they were connected. "The differences," he said, "outweighed the similarities. Susan and Caroline were both abducted on hot July days, in colourful summer clothes; Sarah was abducted on a cold, dark, rainy night in March, her small body covered with an anorak. Both Coldstream and Portobello are on, or near, main roads, commonly used routes through which many travellers pass; Morley is not the sort of place you go without a reason." These facts meant to Clark that whoever took Sarah was likely a local man who knew the area well.

Still, all of the victims (including Sarah) were young girls who had been skillfully kidnapped from public locations, sexually abused, and then disposed of. The suspect drove the victims south, dumped their bodies in the Midlands, and they were found within twenty-six miles of each other. Unique to Sarah's case was the fact her body had been violently treated by her killer. Serial killers often get more aggressive and violent as they kill (such as Peter Sutcliffe). They gain confidence and require more killing to keep their inner voices satisfied. Several detectives in Sarah's case thought her murder was more extreme. They cited the sexual assault and the fact she'd been thrown in the river still alive.

Initially, based on Hector Clark's assumption, Sarah's murder was treated as a separate case. Detective Superintendent John Stainthorpe of the West Yorkshire Police Department, took the lead of Sarah's case. Stainthorpe would look for ways to connect Sarah's case to the other two murders (Maxwell/Hogg), because he sensed a connection between them.

The same painstaking work regarding inquiries, leads, and case discussion took place during the investigation of Sarah's murder. Officers went door to door in the neighborhood and learned that a white van had been parked near Sarah's house prior to her abduction. An artist's impression of a strange man who was seen on the street near Sarah's home and inside the K&M Stores was circulated. LIO's were asked to provide names of possible suspects, which they did. Every name on the list was contacted and interviewed but led to negative results.

Unlike the other two murder investigations, however, Stainthorpe had a tool they didn't: the Home Office Large Major Enquiry System (HOLMES) had been established. The HOLMES system was donated to the West Yorkshire police after the Yorkshire Ripper 'disaster,' and it was used since the beginning of the Sarah Harper murder investigation. The system could efficiently log, process, collate, and compare information with a single inquiry. Once all the data from the investigation had been fed into HOLMES, names of possible suspects or vehicle registration numbers, for instance, could be fed into the system, which would instantly tell the user whether the name or vehicle had come up previously in the investigation. This tool would make searching for a needle in a haystack at least seem possible.

Unfortunately, even though the system was being used and morale was high that a lead would develop, HOLMES was unable to further the police investigation into the murder of Sarah Harper. The major flaw with the system was if the suspect they were looking for was not already in the database, HOLMES would not be able to alert them of who to look for. Stainthorpe hoped the suspect would be in the system, but he was not. He and his team were left with yet another dead end.

Eight months into the investigation of Sarah's murder, Her Majesty's Inspector of Constabulary determined all three cases were, in fact, related and suggested one database be established to investigate the murders. The request sounded easy but was near impossible to implement. The Maxwell investigation was still manually contained, and although the Hogg and Harper cases were fed into a computer database, the two programs could not communicate with each other. This meant all three cases needed to be entered into one program. It required three years to enter all of the data from the three murder cases into one computerised database. Officers investigating the murders of Sarah, Susan, and Caroline were extremely hopeful the computer program might shed light on the investigations and finally provide law enforcement at least one solid lead.

As the data processing continued, so too did the killer. It had been three years since the abduction and murder of Susan

Harper, but police in Stow-on-the-Wold, England, were advised of a kidnapping in progress in their town that was eerily similar to these cases.

Chapter Five

Village Stow, along the Scottish border, July 14, 1990

A sunny yet pleasant day was forming in the village of Stow and families, especially their children, were playing outside taking advantage of amazing weather. Six-year-old Mandy Wilson skipped along toward her friend's house hoping they could play together. As she walked along the street, a neighbor of hers, David Herkes, watched as Mandy approached a white van. For some reason, his mind registered the fact that the passenger door to the van was wide open, but no one was standing near the van.

Curious, he peered over toward the van while checking his lawn mower blades and his heart stopped. "All I could see were her little feet standing next to a mans. Suddenly, they vanished, and I saw him making movements as if he was trying to stuff something under the dashboard. He got into the van, reversed up the driveway the child had just come from, and sped off towards Edinburgh."

David Herkes wrote down the van's registration number and called the police. He provided the van's description and registration number to the dispatch centre, and police swarmed the area trying to rescue a young girl reported being kidnapped.

Herkes told reporters after making the call, "I was standing near the spot where the child had been abducted, briefing the police and the girl's distraught father about what had happened. Suddenly, I saw the van again and shouted 'That's him.' The officer dashed into the road and the van swerved to avoid him before coming to a halt."

Officers surround the van and yank the driver out. He verbally identified himself as Robert Black. They handcuffed him and placed him in a nearby patrol car.

Mandy's father, Mr. Wilson, stated at the time, "I shouted at Black, 'That's my daughter - what have you done to her, you bastard?' But his reaction was nil, he had no expression. I could have got my hands round his throat there and then, but my concern was for my daughter, not him. Where was she? Was she alive or, God forbid, dead? I went straight for a pile of rags just behind the seat and felt a little body inside the sleeping bag... I can't tell you how I felt as I unwrapped her from the bag and saw her little face bright red from the heat and lack of air. She was so terrified as I untied her and took the tape from her mouth that she didn't utter a word."

Robert had tied the little girl's hands behind her back, covered her mouth with Elastoplast, and shoved her into a sleeping bag. Prior to doing so, he'd already sexually assaulted her. Robert later told Ray Wyre during an interview months later, "I pulled her pants to one side and I had a look. I thought I'd just sort of stroke [her vagina]... but there was bruising on the inside - I don't know how." He then told Wyre what he would have done if he had not been caught, "When I'd done the delivery in Galashiels down the road, I would have assaulted Mandy sexually. I would have probably stripped her from the waist down, but I would have untied her and probably took the plaster off her mouth. And if she called out when I was assaulting her, then I might have put the gag back on."

Wyre, quoting Doctor Baird, a well-known doctor who'd also interviewed Robert several times based on his serial killings, noted Robert later said of the incident, 'I would have put things into her vagina to see how big she was. I would have put my fingers in, and also my penis.' When asked about other objects, he agreed he might put other objects into her vagina. When Robert was asked for an example of what other objects he might use, he smiled and stared at Doctor Baird's pen, inferring that he'd use the instrument in a perverse manner.

Robert would sometimes follow these statements by claiming that he loved all children. Wyre asked him how he could do such terrible things to children, especially since he claimed to love them so much. Robert answered, "I wasn't thinking about her at all... like, you know, what she must be feeling." He thought a moment and continued, "If she had died it would have been a pure accident."

Thus Robert had transformed, at least in his mind, his victims from humans into mere objects for his own pleasure. This is typical of many serial killers but Robert appeared also to gain pleasure in his victims' sufferings. These children, then, became an object that he could poke, probe, experiment with, and later get rid of. Nowhere in any of Robert's statements does he recall his victims protesting or resisting his brutality; however, one must assume his victims fought his advances in some manner.

While Robert was being transported to the Selkirk police station, he told officers in the car that the kidnapping was, "A rush of blood," and spontaneously stated, "I have always liked little girls since I was a kid." Robert told police he was going to keep Mandy until his last delivery was complete, and then he, "Would have spent some time with her, maybe in Blackpool." Lastly he told them he planned to let her go once he was finished with her. The officers did not find Robert to be truthful about releasing Mandy. They were certain the keen eye of David Herkes and their ability to act quickly saved Mandy from certain death.

The MO Robert displayed while kidnapping Mandy matched that of the murders of Susan Maxwell, Caroline Hogg, and Sarah Harper. Specifically, the following similarities existed:

- All the victims were young girls.
- All were bare-legged, wearing white ankle socks.
- All were taken from a public place.
- Susan and Caroline were both abducted on hot July days.
- All were abducted in a vehicle of some sort; Susan and Sarah were both abducted in Transit-type vans.
- After abduction, all the victims were taken some miles south.
- All the bodies showed signs of a sexual motive for the attack: "Each victim was obviously taken for sexual gratification. Susan Maxwell's pants were removed, Caroline Hogg was naked and Sarah Harper was found to have suffered injury."
- "None suffered any gross bruising or broken bones."

- Both Susan and Sarah had been unclothed and then re-clothed; all three victims had their shoes removed.

- No real attempt was made to hide the bodies.

- All the bodies had been dumped in what became known to police as the 'Midlands Triangle,' a 26 mile area encompassing parts of Nottinghamshire, Staffordshire, and Leicestershire.

It did not take much time for lead investigator Deputy Chief Constable Hector Clark to meet Robert Black. The meeting and subsequent brief interview proved powerful for Clark. He later recalled, "Slowly he [Robert] looked up at me and my gut feeling was that this was my man. I had always thought that when I saw him I would know him, and every instinct told me this was the guy. I knew by his body smell and his disheveled appearance. Except that he was bald, he was just as I expected." Still, like a rotting onion, there were many layers of Robert Black that required peeling to solve multiple murders.

Chapter Six

Matters in the case against Robert for the kidnapping and sexual assault of Mandy Wilson began in court on August 10, 1990. The evidence in this case was overwhelming, and Robert had been caught in the act. Robert and his attorney understood the case against him was massive and air-tight. Robert entered a plea of guilty based on these facts. As such, the prosecution was still required to provide the facts of the case to the Crown. The Lord Advocate, Lord Fraser, would listen to everything the prosecution had against Robert to complete the preliminary hearing.

The prosecutor argued that Mandy would probably have been dead within an hour had she been kept bound and gagged in the sleeping-bag. Doctor Baird's report (he'd interviewed Robert within days of being apprehended) concluded that Robert was, and would remain, a danger to children. This conclusion, from United Kingdom's foremost expert on serial killers, dealt a significant blow to Robert and his team.

Robert's attorney, Herbert Kerrigan, advised the court that his client admitted to liking little girls, but that he had never acted upon his desires. He also told the court that Robert "just wanted to spend time with Mandy and he did not intend to injure her, [and] certainly not to kill her." Robert enjoyed his talks with Doctor Baird. He nodded his head in agreement when Doctor Baird said he [Robert] should never be around children again. Robert's attorney requested, "Some sort of program to get assistance" for Robert realizing the case against him looked bleak.

The Lord Justice Clerk, Lord Ross, did not believe Robert's story. He stated that Mandy's abduction was "carried out with chilling, cold calculation."

"This was," he said "no 'rush of blood,' as you have claimed. This is a very serious case, a horrific, appalling case." Lord Ross sentenced Robert to life imprisonment and told him that his release would not "be considered until such time as it is safe to do so."

This ruling ensured Robert would be in custody for quite some time. Now it was the job of Hector Clark and literally hundreds of officers to gather and build their case against Robert for the abduction and murders of Susan Maxwell, Caroline Hogg, and Sarah Harper. It would prove to be a daunting task requiring years of work, but the families of the victims, and the public following the cases, demanded results.

Chapter Seven

Unfortunately in law enforcement, "instinct" and your "gut feeling" are not enough to get a conviction. Investigate certain crimes long enough and a second-sense develops, but evidence and probable cause are required to charge someone with a crime. When it comes to murder, every possible lead and piece of evidence is crucial. Some investigators are more open about their ability to "know" their suspect. George Oldfield, the man who led the Yorkshire Ripper investigation, mused that if he were in a room full of people and one of them his suspect, he'd be able to point out the suspect. However, the Yorkshire Ripper case, and hundreds of similar cases, have clearly demonstrated how dangerous it is to assume you know someone. For example, Peter Sutcliffe, interviewed nine times in five years, did not get identified as the ruthless killer.

Hoping to extract some useful or incriminating information regarding the cases of Sarah, Susan, and Caroline, the police felt interviewing Robert again would be the best course of action. They hoped, since a life sentence already hung over his head, he might consider talking with detectives thinking he had nothing to lose.

Officers went to Scotland to interview Robert. In a six-hour interview, he spoke openly about offences for which he had previously been convicted. Robert spoke about a variety of topics, including his one true girlfriend, his strong attraction to young girls, the fact he'd been sexually abused as a child, the fantasies that ran through his mind, and his disturbing masturbation routines. His statements were, at a minimum, shocking to the officers.

Hearing that Robert answered their questions at will, they pressed on and asked him about working for Poster Dispatch and Storage (PDS). Before he could answer, they also asked about his whereabouts when Caroline Hogg had been abducted. Robert abruptly went silent. Police waited a few minutes and asked him about Susan and Sarah. Again, Robert remained silent. Somewhere inside his head, a switch had been flipped. Seeing that Robert had shut down, the officers terminated the rest of their questioning. This investigative technique, really the only thing the police had going for them at the time, proved futile.

Law enforcement, then, would need to build their cases, assuming Robert as the suspect, from scratch. It would require chronicling Robert's life, every moment of every day, in an effort to pinpoint his whereabouts when Sarah, Caroline, and Susan were taken. If they could demonstrate his presence in these locations, they'd have their work cut out to convince a jury that he also took the girls. If they could reasonably do that, they'd have to also demonstrate that Robert killed them. Investigators dug into the last nine years of his life hoping to find clues as to who he really had become. Although it seemed nearly impossible, the investigation teams had no other options.

They knew Robert drove a white van as a delivery driver, and they already knew his work routes were close to the areas where Susan, Sarah, and Caroline had been kidnapped. Work records, receipts from fuel cards, and wage books used by Robert were collected and combed through. The police wanted to paint a picture of Robert's habits and routines, specifically on the days the girls were taken.

If you recall, Susan was abducted in Coldstream on July 30, 1982. Investigators tried to piece together Robert's whereabouts that day. The first issue - that of locating old records - proved almost disastrous for the investigators because when they contacted PDS, they learned the records were recently destroyed. Foul play had been suggested, but the company could show that their policy required the purging of old data. Some of the records were, in fact, gone, but the wage books were still available. Different runs require different payment to the drivers. The records indicated Robert received pay for a run through Coldstream between July 29 and August 4. Susan's abduction occurred during the same time, but to charge him with a crime, investigators would need to narrow down the time Robert had driven through.

Investigators located gas receipts from the company's fuel credit cards. All drivers carried a gas card. With the use of gas receipts, police noticed Robert had been in the Borders area on July 30. Records indicated Robert filled up the white van he used while working just south of Coldstream right before Susan had been abducted, and later north of Coldstream after her abduction. The quickest route between the two stations was the A687, directly through Coldstream. People who worked with Robert told police he did not prefer to take the most direct route (which would be the M6 to the M1) and liked to use the A50 to connect to the M1 because he enjoyed the Midlands area. Susan's body was found by the A518 in Staffordshire, not far from the junction for the A50. Investigators had their first piece of circumstantial evidence connecting Robert to the murder of Susan Maxwell.

Similar work was needed to investigate whether Robert had killed Caroline. If you recall, she was abducted on July 8, 1982. By using wage books and gas receipts, police were able to show that Robert delivered posters to Mills and Allen in Piershill, just over a mile north of Portobello. Gas receipts indicated he filled up in Belford, Northumberland, on the day Caroline went missing. The most direct route from Belford to Piershill went through Portobello. A post-mortem autopsy on Caroline indicated the killer must have kept her for four days after the abduction (they could not determine if she was dead or alive during this time). This meant on July 12th, the fourth day after she went missing, would be the first day the killer could have disposed of her body. Police noticed Robert delivered posters to Bedworth, roughly ten miles from where Caroline's body had been recovered. Again, investigators had more circumstantial evidence connecting Robert to the murder of Caroline Hogg.

Police then looked at the murder case of Sarah Harper. As you will recall, she was abducted on March 26, 1986. PDS records indicated Robert delivered posters to a depot just 150 yards from the place where Sarah had been seen last. Gas receipts from the following day demonstrated Robert drove directly on the A453 to Nottingham, which is where Sarah's body had been recovered. Again, investigators had obtained circumstantial evidence indicating Robert might have been involved in the murder of Sarah Harper.

While Hector Clark and his team dug for more evidence against Robert, another case caught Clark's attention. He noticed on

April 28, 1988, a little girl named Teresa Thornhill had been at a park with her friends. When it was time to go, she walked part of the way home with her friend, Andrew Beeson. At some point they separated. Teresa then noticed that a blue van had stopped just ahead of her on the opposite side of the road. The driver was looking under the vehicle's hood. As she approached, the man shouted to her, "Can you mend engines?" Teresa remembered being scared, replied that she could not, and picked up her pace walking away from the man. Within a few seconds, the same man grabbed her from behind, picked her up, and carried her to his van.

Teresa said of the incident, "I will never forget his hairy arms, sweaty hands, and smelly T-shirt. He came over to me and got me in an all-encompassing bear hug which I could not get out of because he was very strong. I tried to struggle free and began shouting for my mum. I was looking around for something to hit him with, but there was nothing there. Then I grabbed him between the legs." She thrashed about trying to get away from her attacker.

As she continued to struggle, she knocked the attacker's glasses to the ground and began screaming as loud as she could. Andrew, Teresa's friend, heard her screams and ran towards the van shouting, "Get off her, you fat fucking bastard." Teresa continued to fight to free herself while Andrew also joined in trying to release the grasp of her attacker. The suspect, seeing the commotion the two children were causing, dropped Teresa from his clutch, jumped into his van, and fled.

The specifics of this case seemed similar to the murders of Sarah, Susan, and Caroline, at least to lead investigator Hector Clark. Although they'd been between the ages of five and eleven when they were murdered, Teresa was fifteen. However, based on her height, weight, and facial structure, she appeared as young as the other girls. Still, Clark felt this case could be linked to their murders and spent considerable time analysing the case notes. He noticed that Teresa's description of her attacker, and the description of the attacker's van, matched Robert Black completely.

By the end of 1990, law enforcement had accumulated a great amount of circumstantial evidence against Robert, but they still had no forensic evidence or a confession. Hector Clark and his team decided to re-interview Robert armed with the circumstantial evidence they'd gathered. They interviewed him for three days. Robert refused to answer their questions pertaining to the murders of Susan, Sarah, and Caroline. His refusal to reply dealt a significant blow for all of the people involved. Faced with no other option, Mr. Clark decided to write up everything they had collected against Robert for the murders and submit his findings to the Crown.

In May of 1991, Mr. Clark delivered the report to the Crown Prosecution Service. The murder cases rested in their hands now.

In April of 1992, while Robert enjoyed celebrity status in prison, ten summonses were served against him. Clark and the other officers involved in the case were ecstatic that charges were brought against Robert. However, the subsequent court battle would drain all involved and would be somewhat of a circus on the news and in the newspapers.

Chapter Eight

Two years went by before the case against Robert Black, charged with the murders of Sarah Maxwell, Susan Harper, and Caroline Hogg, actually found its way in front of a judge for a preliminary hearing. Investigators turned over twenty-two tons of evidence to the prosecution. The prosecution provided a copy of the evidence to the defense team. The logistics of this task were almost unbearable. Numerous hang-ups and legal technicalities bogged the preliminary process down significantly.

Jurisdictional concerns arose because the cases were committed across two countries. In addition, the prosecution's case relied upon being allowed to present the murders as a series, while Robert's team wanted them presented one at a time. Lastly, the abduction of Mandy Wilson became a significant legal concern. The prosecution needed to present Mandy's case as evidence of Robert's unique MO, whereas his defense team argued the case should not be allowed during the current proceedings. The defense stated that submitting a past offense as evidence of the commission of a present offence (known as similar fact evidence) was unethical and would cause problems in the case. The Crown concluded Robert's past offense with Mandy Wilson was "strikingly similar" to the present murder cases against him. Pre-trial rulings landed in favor of the prosecution, and the case went to trial.

Since most of the crimes occurred in England, the Crown determined England would be the venue for the trial. John Milford, leading for the Crown, began his opening speech at two o'clock on the afternoon on April 13, 1994. Held in the Moot Hall, Newcastle, he had the task of proving that the murders of Susan Maxwell, Caroline Hogg, and Sarah Harper, and the abduction of Teresa Thornhill were all part of a series committed by the same person. Then he needed to convince the jury that Robert Black committed the murders.

No forensic evidence existed. Robert gave no confession. Mr. Milford, therefore, presented the mountain of circumstantial evidence against Robert Black. Robert had been placed at all of the locations where the girls were kidnapped. He was there at the times they were taken. Similarly, Robert had been in the areas where their bodies were recovered and during the time they were discovered. Several witnesses described a man, who they believed to be Robert Black, in the area of the crimes. During the abductions, Robert drove a van matching the one reported at most of the scenes. Controversial, yet damaging, Robert's team admitted the manner and style of how he took Mandy bore striking resemblance to what happened to Sarah, Susan, and Caroline.

Milford highlighted to the jury the similarities between the murders, trying to convince them the same person had committed each one.

- All the victims were young girls.
- All were bare-legged, wearing white ankle socks.
- All were taken from a public place.
- Susan and Caroline were both abducted on hot July days.

- All were abducted in a vehicle of some sort; Susan and Sarah were both abducted in Transit-type vans.

- After abduction, all the victims were taken some miles south.

- All the bodies showed signs of a sexual motive for the attack: "Each victim was obviously taken for sexual gratification. Susan Maxwell's pants were removed, Caroline Hogg was naked, and Sarah Harper was found to have suffered injury."

- "None suffered any gross bruising or broken bones."

- Both Susan and Sarah had been unclothed and then re-clothed; all three victims had their shoes removed.

- No real attempt was made to hide the bodies.

- All the bodies had been dumped in what became known to police as the 'Midlands Triangle', a 26-mile area encompassing parts of Nottinghamshire, Staffordshire, and Leicestershire.

Milford said of the murders, "They are so unusual, the points of similarity so numerous and peculiar, that it is submitted to you that you can safely conclude that they were all the work of one man." Milford argued the one man had to be Robert Black. "The Crown alleges that Robert Black kidnapped each of his victims for sexual gratification, that he transported them far from the point of abduction, and murdered them."

After outlining the similarities in the murders, Milford turned his focus on the charge of the abduction of Teresa Thornhill. First he noted that Teresa was a girl (who looked younger than her 15 years), she'd been grabbed off a busy street in the north of England, by a scruffy looking man, driving a van. Milford told the court that on that very day, Robert delivered posters to a firm in Nottingham in his blue transit van. He also noted the description of the attacker and the van, provided by Teresa, matched Robert and the vehicle he drove that day. Teresa told the police that her attacker smelt strongly; the Rayson children had nicknamed their lodger 'Smelly Bob', and Eric Mould, Robert's former boss at PDS, told the court that his workers used to complain about Robert being dirty and having bad body odor. Milford then noted that while police searched Robert's home after the Mandy Wilson abduction, they found a newspaper clipping of Teresa's attack. He told the Crown that serial killers often kept news clippings and other mementos from their killings like trophies.

As Justice Macpherson ruled Mandy's attack admissible, Milford presented it as evidence against Robert. Milford said that Black had admitted to this abduction and assault and that "it has all the hallmarks of the three murders and the abduction that he now stands trial for." Milford argued the crimes were "virtually carbon copies. At Stow, he was repeating almost exactly what had happened at Coldstream." Milford continued, "The little girl in Stow was wearing shorts when she was taken, was bare-legged and was wearing white socks. She was to be transported many miles south. Again it was the end of the week, it was July, and it was hot. Stow and Coldstream are similar villages only 25 miles apart. Even more remarkably, like Susan Maxwell, the little girl was wearing yellow shorts."

Robert admitted to kidnapping Mandy Wilson. Milford told the jury "this abduction was a 'carbon copy' of that of Susan Maxwell; the abduction of Teresa Thornhill and the abductions and murders of Caroline and Sarah were carbon copies of Susan's abduction; therefore, Robert Black must have committed the three murders."

The prosecution had done well setting the foundation for the case against Robert. The evidence presented assuredly demonstrated a series or pattern in the murders, but the prosecution now needed to convince the jury Robert killed the girls.

Milford turned to the police reports and investigation placing Robert at all the abduction and dumping areas around the times the crimes occurred. Several days were needed to present everything law enforcement had collected in the murders. Milford concluded that Robert was the killer, or a "similarly perverted 'shadow' of Robert was following him around the country." The fact Robert had convictions for sexual assaults on children and a penchant for child pornography only served to lessen the likelihood of a shadow committing the heinous crimes.

Deputy Chief Constable Hector Clark testified last in the case against Robert Black. Clark described the investigation as "the largest crime inquiry ever held in Britain." He cited unfathomable statistics and said the database held details of 187,186 people, 220,470 vehicles, and interviews with 59,483 people. When Milford asked Clark how unusual it was for three children to have been abducted, murdered, and then dumped a relatively long distance away, Clark replied that in his 39-year career as a policeman "I have no knowledge of any other cases with these features." Finally, the case for the prosecution was closed.

Ronald Thwaites would represent Robert Black. He immediately noted the prosecution had no forensic evidence nor did it have any help from the defendant himself (referring to the lack of a confession or statement from Robert). Oddly, Robert and his team did not provide an alibi for his whereabouts during the abductions, and they never initially suggested another individual as a would-be suspect. Thwaites had his hands full with Robert, who'd admitted several times of being a child abductor and molester. Thwaites tried to argue that although his client was "wicked and [a] foul pervert," this alone did not mean necessarily that he was a murderer.

According to Thwaites, Robert had become "a murderer for all seasons," a scapegoat for the desperate police who, after a nine-year investigation, had got no further than from where they had started. "This series of cases," said Thwaites, "reeks of failure, disappointment, and frustration." Thwaites told the jury of Robert's previous convictions and spoke of his pedophilic pornography. Regarding the Mandy Wilson case, Thwaites argued, "the judge saw it fit to give him a life sentence. No one can be surprised by that, and everyone must applaud it. Black's lifelong interest in children is further confirmed by the haul of pornography in his home. It is revolting and sickening to look at." But, he said, "however wicked and foul Black is, and I am not here to persuade you to like him or find any merit in him at all, it is not unreasonable to suppose that there might be some evidence to adorn the prosecution's case other than theory. This case has been developed before you using one incident of abduction, which he admitted, as a substitute for evidence in all these other cases. There is no direct evidence against Black."

The lack of evidence remained Thwaite's focus, and he continued trying to show flaws in the prosecution's case. Even though the prosecution had called James Fraser, of the Lothian and Borders police forensics laboratory, to testify on its behalf, Fraser's testimony marginally helped the defense. He testified that he and six other scientists had spent six months working solely on this case, examining over 300 items belonging to Robert. When Thwaites asked him during cross-examination, "Have you been able to make a scientific link between this man, Black, and any of these murders?"

Fraser replied, "No."

Robert's team then went after law enforcement and the prosecution by concluding they were so certain Robert had committed the crimes that they did not consider other suspects. Thwaites said the Crown had, "tried to match together a new suit made from oddments, but it is full of holes whereas the original suit has been left - until discovered by my team." Thwaites went as far as alleging the true killer of the girls remained at large and his client was innocent.

The defense finally called their star witness, Thomas Ball. Mr. Ball testified that on the day Susan was abducted, he saw a young girl hitting a maroon Triumph with a tennis racket. "She was making quite a lot of noise," he recalled. "It seemed to be a child throwing a fit of temper." He said that there were two or three people inside the car; the driver was a teenager with a wispy beard. When later shown a photograph of Susan by police, Mr. Ball said he was "certain" the photo he was shown matched the girl in the car with the teenage boy. This testimony made it appear perhaps the people in the maroon car had taken Susan, not Robert.

Sharon Binnie, a witness for the defense, explained that she and her husband saw a dark red saloon car like a Triumph 2000 parked in the same place as Thomas Ball described; Joan Jones and her husband had also seen a dark colored car in a lay-by; and Alan Day and Peter Armstrong had similarly seen red saloon cars. Thwaites was hoping to cause doubt in the minds of the jurors with these witness statements.

Michelle Robertson, who was a young girl at the time of the murders, testified about seeing a "scruffy" man in a blue Ford Escort; Kevin Catherall and Ian Collins claimed to have seen red Ford Escorts.

This evidence was useless; however, as the prosecution pointed out, the people in these cars were not noted as doing anything suspicious and were merely in the area during the times the children were abducted.

Lastly, Thwaites attempted to appeal to the jury and told them the only question in this case was whether "it may be proved he [Black] graduated from molester to murderer. There is nothing automatic about that."

"The prosecution," he said dramatically, "Has conducted their case here from beginning to end without letting you into an important secret. The secret is that there is no evidence against Black."

The jury was sent away to deliberate on the case on May 17, 1994. On the third day, the jury agreed on a verdict. Robert Black, who'd been physically and sexually abused as a child, and admitted to the abduction and sexual assault of Mandy Wilson, was found guilty on all counts. The sigh of relief in the courtroom could be heard outside the courtroom.

Justice MacPherson sentenced Robert to life for each of the charges, adding that for the murders, "I propose to make a public recommendation that the minimum term will be 35 years on each of these convictions."

When Robert was escorted away from the court room, he stopped and turned to the large group of officers present to hear the verdict being read and said, "Well done, boys."

The trial and prior investigations cost over £1m (one million pounds), but that is the cost of doing business when it comes to serial killer cases. The guilty verdict meant the families of Sarah, Caroline, and Susan could finally begin the healing process after losing their beautiful little girls to a terrible human being.

Robert is not eligible for parole until 2029, when he will be 82 years old. To this day, he has not admitted to the murders of Susan Maxwell, Sarah Harper, or Caroline Hogg. Their families, however know he is their killer. Somehow, they've tried to pick up the pieces of their difficult and shattered lives.

In his last talk with Ray Wyre, Robert was asked why he never denied the charges against him (Wyre was referring to the murders of Sarah Harper, Susan Maxwell, and Caroline Hogg). Robert paused, looked Mr. Wyre directly in the eyes and said, "Because I couldn't."

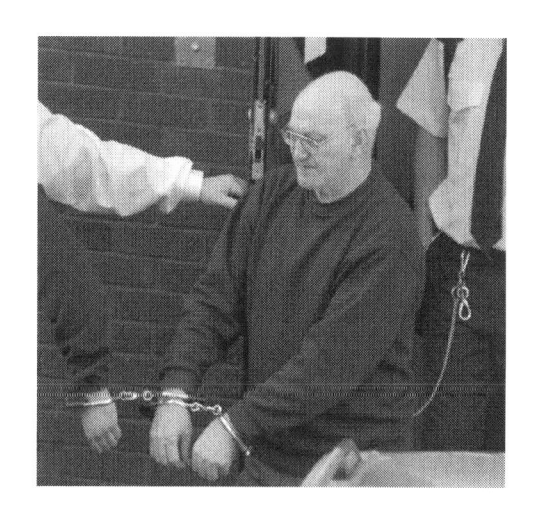

Robert escorted from court, 2010

Robert escorted to court, 1990

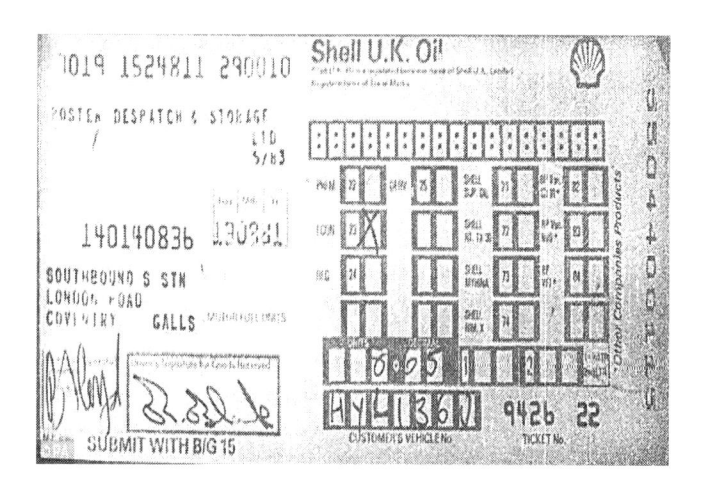

One of Robert's gas receipts used to convict him

A similar van was used in some of the abductions

Chapter Nine

Robert Black, one of the most horrific serial killers in United Kingdom history, had rightfully been convicted, but the public had grown irate that it took such a long period of time to apprehend him. People noted that it took police three years longer to catch Robert than it did Peter Sutcliffe. People following the case pointed at Robert's lengthy previous criminal behavior, the majority of which was sexual in nature, and could not understand how police did not think of him as a suspect until *after* he'd been caught while abducting Mandy Wilson.

Further, various police databases and hundreds of officers were involved, yet no one fingered Robert as a suspect. Police, while under heavy criticism, pointed out several issues: working the murder cases separately for a while, then combining the cases, and finally the task of entering everything into one database. They said the combination and sequence of events were the reason so much time went by before labeling Robert as the suspect. By the time all the work entering the data had been finished, Robert had already been considered a suspect based on the fact the MO he used while abducting Mandy Wilson was so similar to the murders of Susan, Sarah, and Caroline.

During the time the murders were being investigated, Robert had not been interviewed because the computer systems did not include his name. Robert's name was also not in the HOLMES system. Therefore, he'd never been considered a suspect because to the various computer systems, Robert did not exist. The software used in the computer databases were fairly accurate, but only as good as the data the police included.

Local media and several law enforcement members directed their criticism at Deputy Chief Constable Hector Clark. Detective Superintendent John Stainthorpe, who had headed the Sarah Harper investigation initially, said Clark defined his parameters too narrowly when looking at men with records for sexual offences as potential suspects. Clark searched for men who had been convicted of serious sexual offences, which left out

Robert's sexual act with the seven-year-old victim in Scotland in 1967. Stainthorpe said if Clark would have included all sexual offenses, Robert would have been labeled as a possible suspect, and at the very least, been entered into the computer system and interviewed. He went as far as to state, "Black should have been arrested years ago, with his history and convictions."

Clark quickly defended himself and offered in rebuttal, "We just couldn't check on everybody." He continued, "It would have overloaded the system to an unmanageable extent." He maintained that investigating murderers required research into suspects who committed serious sexual offences because those subjects were more likely to commit murder. Thus, crimes like Robert had committed were not included and exposed a massive flaw in Clark's reasoning.

Serial killers oftentimes do not have serious crime convictions in their past, and some have none for sexually-related crimes. For example, Ian Brady, Colin Ireland, Fred West, and John Christie had minor offenses (fraud, theft, breaking and entering) in their past. Likewise, Dennis Nilsen, Peter Sutcliffe,

Rose West, and Myra Hindley had no criminal records before their convictions for multiple murders. Robert, though, became a serial killer and also a pedophile, a disturbing yet unique blend. Pedophiles normally have past convictions for sexual offenses, although many are minor.

If the investigation, as Stainthorpe suggested, included these minor previous convictions, the amount of data would have undoubtedly slowed the entire process. The number of offenders over a twenty-year period who committed minor offenses or minor sexual crimes would have been astronomical. Therefore, in some small sense, Clark had to choose somewhere to cut the line. He chose to focus on serious offenders. Unfortunately, this decision kept Robert at large for quite some time. It should also be noted that at the time, no computer system existed for this kind of inquiry. In addition, there were not enough police officers in the country to handle the work load these cases would have generated if every person who committed such crimes had been contacted and interviewed.

The Peter Sutcliffe case confirmed the need for computers to assist in complex investigations. The HOLMES system did get used, but only after a long period of time slipped by as police and analysts inputted the accumulated data. At the time, the investigators had nothing like FBI's VICAP system, which includes sex offenders and their MO's. John Stainthorpe noted, "Had Black been on a computerised criminal intelligence system, his name would have popped up like a cork out of a bottle." It was a bold statement at the time, but fairly accurate.

With Robert's case, a system like VICAP would have identified Robert as a potential lead or suspect based on his convictions for sexual assaults, especially since his victims were young girls. The system might also have indicated crimes he may have done but was not yet linked to, which might have tied the murder investigations into the failed abduction of Teresa Thornhill. Investigators would have interviewed Robert and his past would have caught up with him. This alone would have steered police toward Robert and made it much quicker to identify him as the suspect, and no doubt prevented murders.

Chapter Ten

After the convictions in the murders of Susan, Sarah, and Caroline, investigators felt Robert Black and the MO he deployed made him a possible suspect for several unsolved murders. The victims in the cases were eerily similar to the ones he'd been found guilty of killing.

In 1994, a meeting of investigators took place in an effort to determine whether or not Robert could be a suspect for murders in Germany, Ireland, Amsterdam, and France. At least eight known unsolved kidnappings and murders in England exist with striking resemblance to Robert's MO: April Fabb taken off her bicycle in Norfolk in 1969; nine-year-old Christine Markham grabbed in Scunthorpe in 1973; 13-year-old Genette Tate who went missing in Devon in 1978; 14-year-old Suzanne Lawrence found dead in Essex in 1979; 16-year-old Colette Aram found strangled and sexually assaulted in a field in Nottingham in 1983; and 14-year-old Patsy Morris found dead near Heathrow in 1990.

One senior officer at the meeting has been quoted as saying, "We know he [Robert Black] killed Genette Tate and April Fabb, and we believe their bodies are buried somewhere in the Midlands Triangle." These two cases remain open; however, Robert has not been officially tied to the cases or charged in any crime associated to their cases.

John Stainthorpe stated he believed an eighty percent probability existed that Robert was involved in the disappearance of Genette Tate. Although local law enforcement believes Robert killed these girls, no evidence exists suggesting he did, and he's never admitted to killing them. Some locals, particularly the Tate and Fabb families, have wondered if the police, by focusing solely on Robert for the murders of their children, are allowing the true killer to remain free. It's a valid point, and as of now, we have no way of knowing whether or not this is true.

Genette Tate, 1978

April Fabb

On April 8, 1969, at approximately 1:40 p.m., thirteen-year-old April Fabb rolled her bicycle from the front of her house, climbed on, and began riding toward her sister's house in Roughton. In the saddlebag on her bike was a packet of cigarettes. She planned to give the cigarettes to her brother-in-law as a birthday present.

At approximately 2:00 p.m., witnesses noted they saw her riding her bike along a country road, still in the direction of Roughton.

At approximately 2:15 p.m., two Ordinance Survey workers located a blue and white girl's bicycle in a field along the path April had ridden. After careful consideration and examination by her parents, investigators learned the bicycle belonged to April. The Norfolk Constabulary police opened a missing person investigation but were worried something terrible had happened to April.

Numerous people volunteered to help search for April, but no trace of her existed. To this day, the reason for her disappearance remains labeled as unknown.

In 1997, thermal imaging cameras were used to search large fields and areas along roads in the Midlands area - the same area where Susan Maxwell, Sarah Harper, and Caroline Hogg were located. The results were negative.

In 2010, based on tip from a local resident claiming that April's remains were dumped in a well, several wells were excavated. The results were negative again. This case remains open, but Robert Black has not been charged with any crime relating to April.

April Fabb, 1969

Christine Markham

On May 21, 1973, nine-year-old Christine Markham left her home on Robinson Road in Scunthorpe, United Kingdom, and within minutes disappeared. Thousands of statements were taken and at least five thousand homes were searched. The results were negative.

In 2006, Detective Superintendent Christine Wilson and Telegraph Reporter Richard Sharpe re-opened the missing person case of Christine Markham in an effort to find new clues or develop leads.

Police considered digging up the woods near Metheringham, along the Lincolnshire countryside, based on an anonymous letter they received. The letter claimed a relative of the person writing the letter helped dispose of evidence related to Christine's disappearance in the woods. However, no one could corroborate the claim, and the digging did not occur.

A general thermal scoping of the area was conducted, however. Area specialists and archeologists were called in to analyze the data from the scope results. They, along with the police, believed digging in the area and leveling the trees would likely not reveal any positive results pertaining to the whereabouts of Christine.

Detective Sergeant Wilson said of the digging, "When people bury a body, they generally dig where it is easy, but where it was easy to dig thirty years ago, would not be the same today." She added, "If Christine was buried in those woods, the area now has trees growing that were not there thirty years ago, and ground levels have changed.

The search for Christine Markham continues to this day. Police and her family assume she is dead. In 2004, Robert Black was considered a suspect in her disappearance and was questioned at length. Without going into great detail, the police actually confirmed Robert is not a suspect in her case.

Markham family retracing steps after Christine went missing

Suzanne Lawrence

On July of 1979, in Harold Hill, Essex, fourteen-year-old Suzanne Lawrence was reported missing by her parents. They told the police that she left her sister's (their other daughter's) home after telling her (Susanne's sister) to tell her parents she'd be home later. She never made it home, and her body has never been found.

However, her case has been linked to serial killer and sex offender Peter Tobin, who killed young girls and women across Britain while working odd-jobs from the late 1960's to the early 1990's. Robert Black has been eliminated as a suspect in this case as well.

Colette Aram

On October 30, 1983, at approximately 8:00 p.m., Colette Aram left her home in Normanton Lane, Keyworth, to walk one and a half miles to her boyfriend's house. At approximately 8:10 p.m., someone saw her turning into Nicker Hill, where she stopped to talk to a group of friends.

Shortly thereafter, a witness reported hearing a woman screaming followed by a car speeding off shortly afterwards. At approximately 10:30 p.m., Colette's boyfriend reported that she had not arrived as planned. Her family and friends began looking for her near Nicker Hill and near her boyfriend's house.

The following day, at approximately 9 a.m., Colette's naked body was found dumped in a field, about a mile and a half from where she had been abducted (Nicker Hill). She had been raped and strangled to death.

Police launched a murder investigation upon examining Colette's body. On June 7, 1984, the rape and murder of Colette was featured on the newly launched BBC television series *Crimewatch*, a program that reconstructed major unsolved crimes hoping to gain information from viewers. As a result of the show, over four hundred tips came in. Police interviewed and eliminated 1,500 suspects, but the killer remained free. The case was featured for a second time on Crimewatch's 20th anniversary show in

2004. Again, many leads came about, but no suspect was identified.

In 2008, advances in forensic technology allowed the Nottinghamshire Police to put together a DNA profile of the killer. At the same time, the police department asked the public to come forward with names of suspects who would then provide DNA to be eliminated from the case.

Eventually, based on the protocol of collecting DNA swabs on all arrests, DNA was taken from a young man named Jean-Paul Hutchinson. He'd been stopped for a driving violation and subsequently arrested. His DNA was almost a perfect match for the DNA of the person who'd killed Colette; however, based on his age, he could not have been the killer because he had not been born when police discovered the gruesome murder scene. Nevertheless, since the DNA matched Jean-Paul so closely, investigators turned toward looking at his father, Paul Stewart Hutchinson, as a possible suspect. Within a week, Paul Hutchinson was arrested for Colette's murder and later pled guilty. This, then, eliminated Robert as a suspect in her killing.

Patsy Morris

On June 16, 1980, Patsy Morris, while on a school lunch break at Feltham Comprehensive School near Hounslow Heath, essentially vanished from school grounds. No one recalled seeing or hearing anything suspicious and no one saw her walk off campus.

On June 18, 1980, Patsy Morris's body was found face down in a nearby wooded area. Her body is half naked, her underwear was pulled down to her ankles, and her hands were tied. Investigators determined she was raped and violently strangled with one leg of her tights. No attempt had been made to hide her body, and no DNA was found at the scene.

Since then, two individuals were connected to her murder, both by way of confession. On April 12, 2008, Levi Bellfield confessed that he killed Patsy. Bellfield, convicted of killing two people just prior to this statement, said he and the victim dated around the time of her death. Bellfield had no way to confirm the claim, and the police eventually ruled him out as Patsy's killer.

On April 17, 2008, another suspect walked into a police station and confessed to killing Patsy. The suspect was arrested but later released on bail. Police reported that the subject had significant mental health issues and they were unsure how valid his claim to having killed Patsy was. At this time, no known information connects Robert Black to her case. And, after careful consideration and examination of the evidence available, her crime did not fit the MO Robert used during his murders.

Chapter Eleven

Since Robert's conviction, the families of his victims have openly expressed their gratitude toward law enforcement and the Crown for apprehending and helping convict Robert. Some of the family members of the victims have been interviewed after the ordeal and have shared their feelings; some of their views might be considered surprising. Likewise, family members of the missing girls - believed to have been killed by Robert Black - still sought answers and their own closure.

Phillip Cardy, the brother of Jennifer Cardy, spoke in an interview with BBC and said his family did not hate the killer [Robert Black].

"I guess as a family we pity him. I can't hate him and I don't know why. I've tried to muster up a hate, but I don't have it," said Phillip Cardy.

"We did pray for him and for his salvation. I wish he would have asked for forgiveness."

Phillip, six years old at the time Jennifer was kidnapped, said they have not let "Black destroy them."

"You can only forgive somebody once they ask for forgiveness, and if he had done that, we really would have forgiven him," he said.

"I'm very thankful that it's over, because it has been a nightmare, and it is hard to be emotionally strong."

Phillip's sister, Victoria Cardy, was a baby when her sister went missing.

"Although I never knew Jennifer, I know what a hole it left in our family," she said.

Andy and Pat Cardy, Jennifer's parents, said while outside the courtroom when he was convicted, "It has been an emotional couple of hours. It has been a long, long journey. It has been 30 years of a journey," Andy Cardy said.

"We are very, very pleased. We think that justice has been done. We don't think Robert Black will ever be out of jail again to assault little girls."

They listened as Justice Weatherup told Black, "Your crime was particularly serious. You subjected a vulnerable child to unpardonable terror and took away her life."

John Tate, the father of Genette Tate, who went missing 33 years ago, pleaded with the Crown to be allowed to meet Robert.

On August 19, 1978, Genette, thirteen years old at the time, went missing while doing her paper round in a Devon village.

Her bicycle and scattered newspapers were found in a ditch in Aylesbeare, a few minutes after she'd been talking with friends.

Roughly 7,000 volunteers assisted police as they searched for Genette in the village common. Ponds and wells within a 15-mile radius of the village were also dredged, but her body was never found.

John Tate was very sick at the time of his request (2011) and hoped he could ask

Robert directly if he killed his daughter. He said, "I'd like to get this out of the way before I die."

Devon and Cornwall Police have questioned Robert several times over Genette's disappearance, but he continues to deny any involvement with her case.

None of John's requests to meet Robert were answered.

Genette Tate, still missing (considered murdered)

Mr. Tate wrote, "Dear Robert Black, would you make the necessary arrangements for me to be able to visit you. I'd like to come and talk to you."

John said he'd ask Robert, "Did you do it? Did you kill Genette and if so, please can you put us out of our misery and tell us what happened and where?"

He continued, "if he hasn't done it, let's know so we can continue searching for whoever did do it."

Living in Manchester now, John recently went to Aylesbeare on the anniversary of his daughter's disappearance. He laid flowers at a memorial stone for her. It was an emotional event.

The words on the stone say, "Genette Louise Tate. Who disappeared from this village, August 19th 1978. Aged 13 years. Never Forgotten. Always Loved. May she someday be returned to this place to rest in peace."

"It's basically to have a place to be quiet and think," he said. "That's what I use it for anyway, somewhere to come to and just think in the village. Just be at peace."

Detective Sergeant Jane Williams, of Devon and Cornwall Police, said, "Initially it was always considered that Genette had been abducted but, as the years have gone on, both Genette's family and ourselves have had to accept that Genette has probably been murdered."

The force has tried to break the case open since 1978, and still has hundreds of files relating to it, including 20,000 filed cards. These cards still need to be examined.

In 1996 and 1998, law enforcement officers attempted to interview Robert regarding the disappearance of Genette. Robert denied any involvement.

In 2003, detectives went to Belfast to discuss similarities between Genette's disappearance and the murder of Jennifer Cardy. Both forces agreed to work the cases together and they re-interviewed Robert.

In Jennifer's case, she'd gone out on her new red bicycle to visit a friend. The date was August 12, 1981. Jennifer never made it to her friend's house, and her bike was located nearby.

Police in Devon sent a file to the Crown Prosecution Service seeking charges against Robert Black for the murders of Jennifer Cardy and Genette Tate. In 2008, the Crown refused to file against Robert citing the primary reasons as "insufficient evidence."

To this date, Mr. Tate still does not know the fate of his daughter. He, as with many parents of missing children, never had the opportunity to fill the void in his wounded heart.

Mr. and Mrs. Fabb passed away in 2010 and 2013 respectively, also not knowing the fate of their daughter. It does not appear Robert will comment on her abduction.

Chapter Twelve

Right now, Robert Black sits in a concrete cell twiddling his thumbs without a care in the world. He possesses, in that deranged and demented mind of his, the ability to solve or shed light on numerous missing children cases throughout the United Kingdom and various other nearby countries. For some unknown reason, he refuses to admit to any previous kidnappings or murders, yet those who have interviewed him or investigated his cases are certain he left behind far more victims.

I'd never say I feel sorry for Robert Black, but one must admit his life has been quite unique - even troubling - in some respects. His biological mother, Jessie Hunter Black, gave him up as a baby. She also refused to list his biological father on the birth certificate, making it impossible for Robert to ever know his real father. She did not do this because she somehow knew who Robert would become, but rather, in Scotland and most civilized societies in 1947, having children out of wedlock was a major embarrassment and highly frowned upon by society.

That Robert ended up being raised by much older foster parents, both of which are believed to have physically abused Robert, only magnified his odd and unstructured socialization. Then, at a very young age, the only father figure he had, Jack Tulip, died. His foster mother, Margaret, died a few years later leaving Robert at the hands of the community to raise him. They were not prepared for such a task.

Around the time Jack died, Robert began experimenting with his body sexually. It is not known whether this exploration was Robert's way of filling a void, but it certainly, based on his own admissions, happened often and got progressively worse. This exploration, and the subsequent fantasies, festered in Robert's mind until his thoughts deteriorated. He had no one to share these thoughts with, and likely felt no one gave a damn about him.

Bouncing around from boys' homes was one of the worst things for a child, especially during their formative years. As noted, a male staff member sexually abused Robert around the age of twelve. Imagine your biological mother giving you up, your abusive foster parents dying while you're young, and landing in a home where a male staff member forces you to perform sexual acts on him. It is my belief that Robert had no chance of being a normal member of society after facing these monumental challenges.

Robert began to treat young girls as objects, not people, and repeatedly violated them sexually without recourse. The powers that be simply moved him from place to place instead of addressing his fetish for sexually perverse acts. His appetite for his own sexual perversions, most notably his fascination of placing objects in his anus, became a plague to spread throughout society. Robert said he loved his victims, but ended up violating and killing them. Obviously his ability to process how terrible he'd become did not exist.

One single event - when Robert was seventeen - played over and over in his head and is highly attributed to his motive for kidnapping, sexually abusing, and killing four young girls. When he was seventeen, he lured a seven-year-old girl to an abandoned building, choked her out, and masturbated next to her unconscious body. He ejaculated on her, then left her, not knowing if she was dead or alive. He ended up getting charged with this atrocious act, but received minimal punishment. The image, however, of what happened in the abandoned building with the victim haunted Robert, and he tried to relive similar incidents to get the image out of his head, away from his thoughts.

Somehow, Robert meandered through his young adult hood, found various jobs, and assimilated - although as a misfit - into society. He was considered a good employee, learned a deep appreciation for the game of darts, and had a girlfriend named Pamela Hodgson.

Robert fell madly in love with Pamela and asked her to marry him after dating for less than a year. Pamela said yes, but later left him abruptly. She never provided a reason. Leaving Robert instantly crushed him and he would never recover. Only after the breakup did Robert move from his deviant sexual acts with girls to killing multiple children. He would later say, after being served with three murder charges, that Pamela had nothing to do with his behavior. Why make the statement if she in fact had nothing to do with what he did, who he became?

Around the same time Pamela left him, Robert learned his biological mother had married and he had half-siblings, but she never wanted his birth to be known or for Robert to meet his siblings. This, too had to be a significant blow to Robert's inner being. As is the case with several serial killers, the culmination of these events, and the years of sexual abuse he'd done and been the victim of, caused him to snap. In doing so, pure sexually driven rage escaped from him, consuming the lives of four innocent victims.

Although law enforcement presented a monumental case against Robert, the fact is, the evidence was circumstantial. Nevertheless, he was convicted in the murders of Susan Maxwell, Caroline Hogg, Sarah Harper, and Jennifer Cardy. Mandy Wilson, by the grace of God and the astute observations of a nosy neighbor, survived her abduction by Robert. Based on her tenacity, fierceness, and the fact her friend aggressively interfered, Teresa Thornhill also survived the attempted abduction by Robert Black.

There really is no telling how many more victims Robert left in his wake, but until he speaks about what he's done, none of us will know for certain. Those who play chess know predicting or calculating the opponent's next move is vital to becoming victorious. Robert is staring at a board calculating when, or if, he'll choose to play another game with law enforcement. Until fate decides the outcome, I pray for the souls of the little girls who have been missing for generations and hope the void in Robert Black's heart ultimately consumes him.

About the Author

Chris Swinney is a Police Officer in the San Francisco Bay area. His writing includes the bestselling '*Bill Dix Detective Series*' which he based the books on his experience as a cop.

Swinney has written two true crime books for Crimes Canada:

Robert Pickton: The Pig Farmer Killer and *The Killer Handyman: The True Story of William Patrick Fyfe*.

Chris is a big time supporter of Teachers, Parents, Law Enforcement, Doctors, Nurses, Firefighters, American Troops, Juvenile Diabetes Research, and children. He spends time volunteering for his church, at schools, he coaches, and every once in awhile he gets to go fly fishing.

Visit Chris's page at:
rjparkerpublishing.com/c-l--swinney.html

Acknowledgments:

An investigator cannot hope to learn or locate every piece of evidence in a case by his or her self. Without the assistance of eager individuals, with similar goals, many cases would reach "cold case" shelves never to see light again. As such, I'd like to thank the following people, associations, and groups for assisting me with the collection of data for this book. Together, we created a worthwhile read in the hopes of educating others about serial killers. We may never fully understand why they do what they do, but we can try to immerse ourselves in their lives in an effort to prevent further tragedies.

Law Enforcement:
Northumberland Police Department
Staffordshire Police Department
Edinburgh Police Department
Robert Stalker, Superintendent Edinburgh PD
Leicestershire Police Department
Gloucestershire Police Department
Ray Wyre (Posthumously from his extensive

interviews with Robert. He was the pioneer of treatment of sexual offenders in the United Kingdom)

Detective Superintendent John Stainthorpe

Deputy Chief Constable, Hector Clark

Justice Weatherup, Judge, Jennifer Cardy case.

David Spens, Robert's Attorney for Cardy case.

Toby Hedworth, Prosecutor, Cardy case.

David Herkes, eyewitness of an abduction by Robert.

Families:

Liz and Fordyce Maxwell (Susan Maxwell's parents).

Mr. and Mrs. Cardy (Jennifer Cardy's parents).

Annette and John Hogg (Caroline Hogg's parents).

Mr. and Mrs. Wilson (Mandy Wilson's parents)

Acquaintances:

Colin McDougal: Knew Robert as a child.

Jimmy Mannes: Knew Robert as a child.

Michael Collier: Former landlord of Baring Arms Pub, in Islington, where Robert played darts.

Eddie and Kathy Rayson: Provided Robert a room while he was in Stamford Hill.

Research:
BBC News (also www.bbcnews.com)
South London Press
Norfolk Constabulary
Daily Telegraph
The Scotsman
Scunthorpe Telegraph
The Telegraph
The Times
The Guardian
The Independent
The Observer
Wikipedia.com
Murderpedia.com
Crimelibrary.com
Anna Gekoski (Article on Robert Black)